# Mrs Owen's Intermediate Prepper Guide for Women

## Laughing At The Days To Come

By

Katie Owen

Mrs Owen's Intermediate Prepper Guide for Women

SBN-13: 978-1508546764

ISBN-10: 1508546762

*For Tuck, as always*

# TABLE OF CONTENTS

# INTRODUCTION

As I write this, there are horrific new atrocities playing out each day in the news. Many of my Christian women friends are stunned and frightened by the world news as it keeps rolling in week after week. Yet, I have chosen to subtitle Book Two "Laughing at the Days to Come."

I take my comfort and inspiration from the Bible. The wonderful, "perfect" woman of Proverbs 31 did not lead a perfect life. She, like all of us, had to work hard for her family's welfare. Life, even, in the best of times, presents problems. In the worst of times, the "perfect wife" of Proverbs 31 can be overcome with a sense of helplessness, if she has not thought in advance to "the needs of her household." The key is to "think ahead."

*****

*"But as for you, Daniel, conceal these words and seal up the book*

*until the end of time; many will go back and forth, and*

<u>*knowledge will increase.*</u>*" Daniel 12:4 NASB*

The increase in knowledge, easy access to round-the-clock news, weather reports 10 days in advance, the ever-increasing national debt (closing in on 19 trillion dollars as I write this), can be a curse. The knowledge can lead to depression and a feeling of hopelessness. Well, fight it. Your husband and children (and grandchildren) are relying on you, whether they know it or not, to be prepared for whatever may come!

Looking to the future with joy; laughing at the days to come. The increase in knowledge can also be a blessing and is one way the Lord is encouraging you to plan, not fear. The fearful are those without a plan. I hope you are already implementing my advice in Book One. If you are just getting started you can certainly begin here, but I encourage you to read Book One (Mrs. Owen's Beginning Prepper Guide For Women) because it contains some fundamental advise, instructions, and lists not included in Book Two.

So, despite the "news", let's continue to grow that common sense that God gave us. The ONLY way to "laugh at the days to come" is to be prepared for them.

I begin this first chapter with pretty toilets. This should get you on the right track to laughing and not crying at the days to come. REMEMBER: You don't need to take notes. I'll put all the instructions, recipes, websites, etc. in the Appendix listed chapter by chapter. So, just read, absorb and enjoy.

Ready? Let's get goin'!

# CHAPTER ONE

## PRETTY CHAIRS

### (Toilet in Disguise!)

I can just hear y'all sayin', "What?" Yep. Read on and enjoy the pictures:

In Book One: Mrs. Owen's Beginning Prepper Guide For Women, I explained how to make a simple and efficient toilet using a five gallon bucket and a foam pool noodle. This bucket toilet is just fine and a HUGE beginning prep. It is also lightweight, portable, and extremely cheap. So cheap that every member of your group can have their own. None of us want to begin any time of tribulation/long-term off grid living without a nice seat to sit on to do our "bidness" as my Gram used to say.

NOTE: Read the full instructions on this basic and comfortable toilet in Book One.

Well, anyone that knows me knows that one of my favorite phrases is "Aesthetics are everything!" Ok, maybe not *everything*, but a lot. As my readers know, I worry about keeping my family, not just alive, but happy. So, morale is important. For me, aesthetics (i.e.: beautiful surroundings) are key.

The other thought I have about toilets is that you probably don't want a five gallon bucket sitting inside your one room cabin looking like what it is: a toilet.

So, with Tucker, my husband, looking on with a smirk, I came up with an idea that's all mine. I turn wooden chairs into toilets and then disguise them with calico or some other pretty fabric and a cushion. Can't imagine it? That's ok. Neither could Tucker.

Here's a picture of a finished "Katie Owen's toilet."

It's so funny seeing folks, visiting our little cabins for the first time, take a seat on the most comfortable looking chair in the room, not knowing it is our "facility."

NOTE: We pretty much only use the inside chair toilet at night. No one wants to go outside at night, especially us girls. And please don't imagine that the bucket below the chair stays full. For my interior chair toilet, (which only gets used during the night), I empty it in the morning into our outside composting toilet bucket. The outside toilet does keep its contents until about ¾ full of waste and kitty litter or sawdust. Then it gets put into the woods to compost (in the bucket) and the noodle on it gets put onto a new bucket.

*********

Here's my step by step of the process. I'll include all of this information and the pictures again in the Appendix. No need to take notes. I've done it for you. Here are the "ingredients":

1. Find wooden chair that will make a good candidate for a toilet. (That sentence looks funny even to me!)

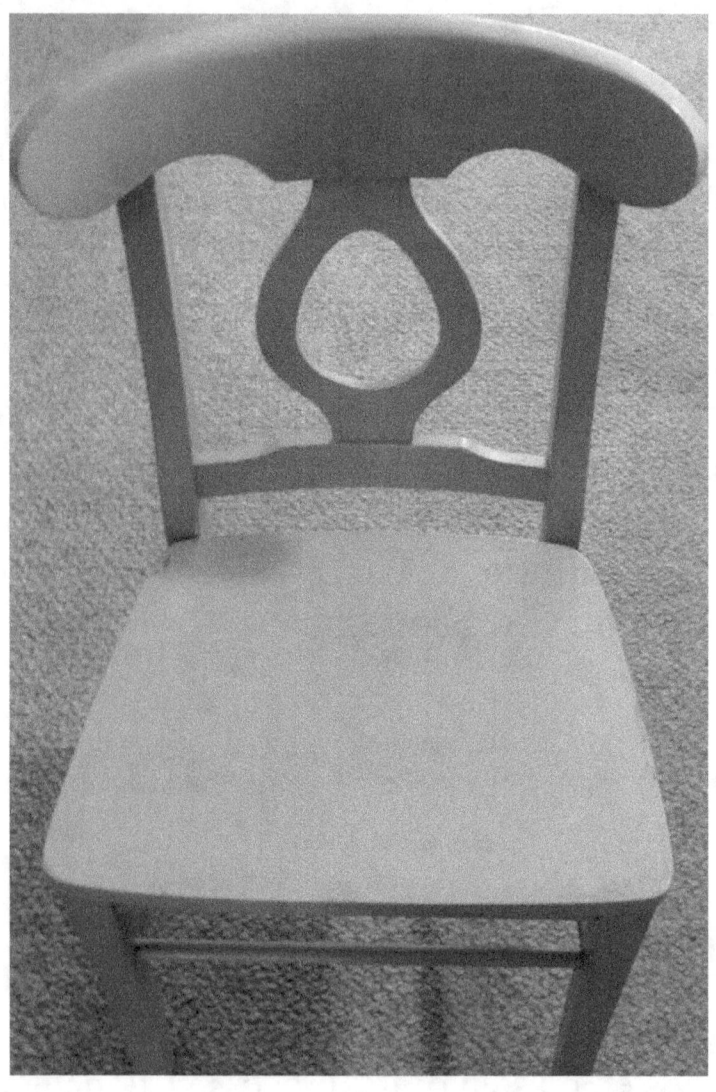

A "good candidate" is one whose seat height is at least 15 inches from the floor to the bottom of the seat. The height should not be more than 20 inches or the "waste" will have to drop a bit too far down. Also, the chair seat itself must be at least 13 inches round, square, or rectangle. In other words, make sure that if the seat is removed you can drop a five gallon bucket down the middle of it without the bucket getting stuck. (LOL, as I write this, I'm sitting in Starbucks eying their "good candidate" chairs and plotting my next toilet!)

NOTE: I've given this a lot of thought and you can use furniture items other than chairs. How about a side table whose dimensions fit the "good candidate" above? Or even a stool. Granted the stool would need to be short and wide, but I've seen them. Shop the thrift stores. You'll find lots of candidates.

Our side table would be a great candidate:

2. A five gallon bucket (sold at all hardware stores and Wal-Mart for a few dollars. (No swim noodle is needed for the chair toilet)
3. A toilet seat. Be sure to get the "standard" size, not the fancy elongated kind. I paid $5.00 at Wal-Mart
4. Three yards of any fabric you think is pretty.
5. Stuffing, quilt batting, or a fleece throw (Again, about $5.00 at Wal-Mart) for the cushion. This cushion, made with the same fabric or a contrasting fabric, will be the last thing you make to lay over the toilet seat and thus, disguise the true function of your chair.
6. Two bungee cords.
7. A package of elastic
8. Upholstery nails (also known as decorative nails or thumbtacks)
9. A sewing machine or a sewing needle with thread.

NOTE: This project may seem too frivolous for some serious-minded "doomsday preppers". While not strictly as "prepper" as a simple bucket or even a hole in the ground (both of which will do the job), this chair is so aesthetically pleasing in your home/cabin environment that it can become a stepping stone to creating a comfortable and comforting oasis. And, after all, this is a book for women!

This chair toilet takes about 2 hours start to finish. Take a look at the step by step pictures I've provided and you will see how fun it was.

To Begin:

1. Take off the seat part of your chair. Most chair seats are simply screwed in place under the seat.

2. Place the entire toilet seat and top on the chair base.

Note: Depending on the opening, you may need to fasten some wood strips in place to make the opening smaller. If you are working with a side table you will need to draw an opening on the top (the same size as the opening in your toilet seat) and use a jig saw to cut the opening.

3. Now attach your toilet seat to the back of your chair using bungee cords.

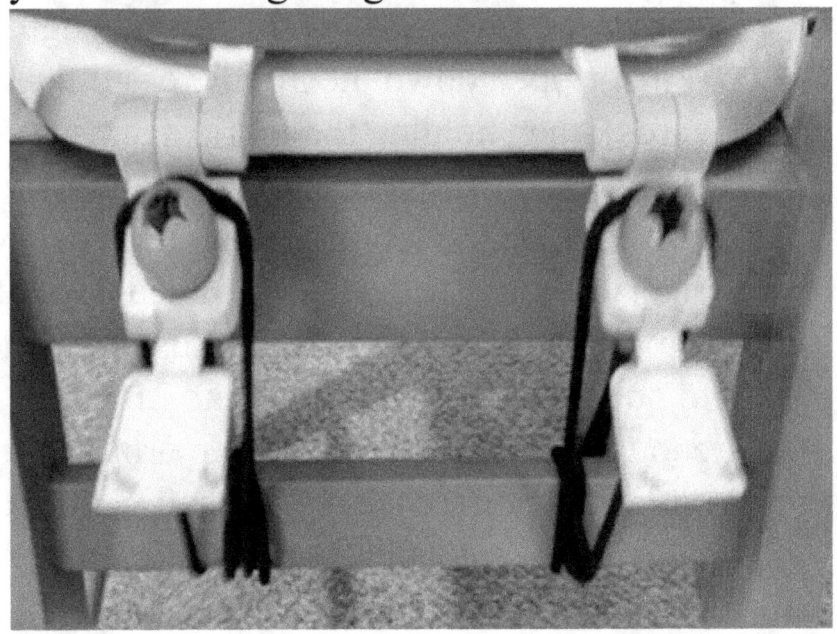

4. That's it, except for placing the bucket (that has an inch or more of sawdust or kitty litter

inside the bottom) on the floor under the chair! Now comes the fun part! The decorating! Yep! We Proverbs 31 women preppers love to embellish!

The first chair I got was already painted a pretty green, so I did not paint it. However, that would be the next step if the color or finish is not to your liking.

First thing I did was cut my fabric lengthwise (I just ripped down the middle of all three yards), then holding the fabric against the chair seat area I pinned down, then ironed, the raw edge on the top (about an inch for my chair) so that I had a clean, folded edge at the top. I made the fabric length just long enough to puddle a bit on the floor and just wide enough (about 1 ½ times to go around the entire circumference of the chair). I did this to give it a full, country-gathered look. I then measured the elastic to the measurement of the circumference of the seat area and took off about three inches to give it some stretch.

NOTE: If my instructions sound hazy, just take a look at the pictures. Hopefully, the pictures will make the "how to" crystal clear. All the instructions and pictures are repeated in the Appendix.

Using my sewing machine, I folded the two short ends of the skirt and sewed down the fold to hide any raw edges. The, using a lot of pins, I zigzagged the stretched elastic around the inner (wrong side) edge.

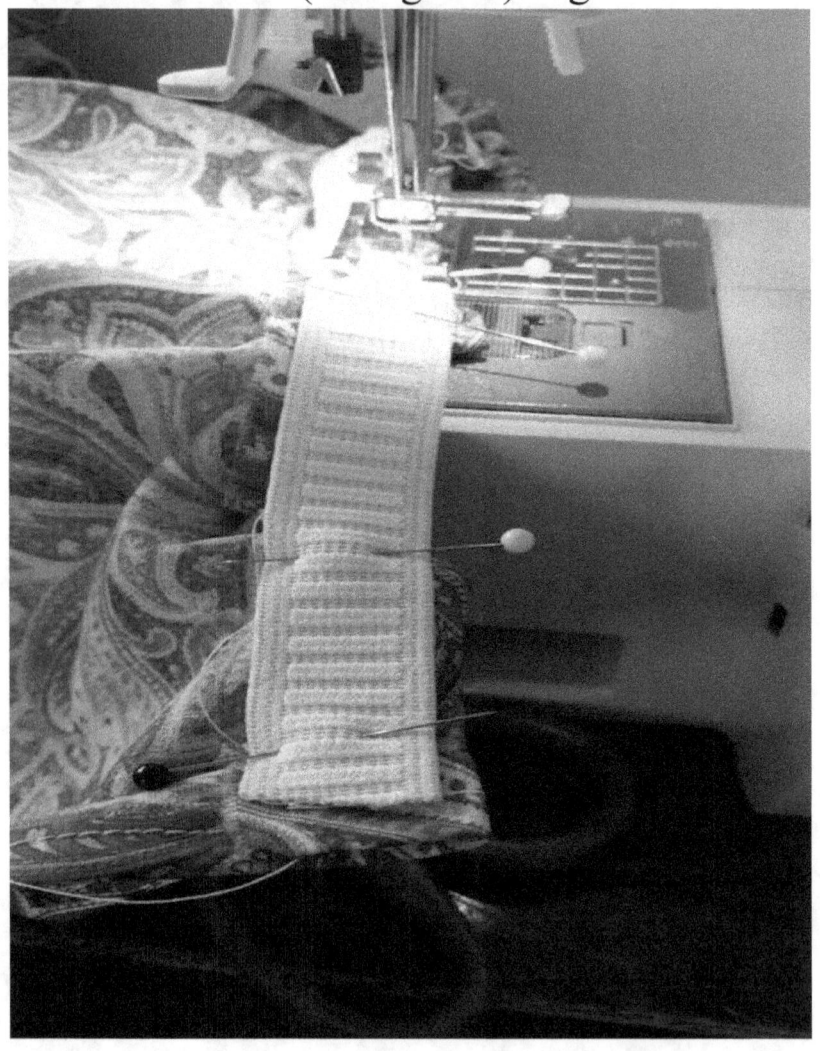

Once you've sewed the elastic to the skirt it is done!

Now take those tacks and little hammer and beginning at the back, tack the skirt onto the outer edge of the chair seat area. I started with two tacks in the back where the two folded over edges meet. (This is the flap opening to access your bucket.) We also use the bucket handle to hold the toilet paper out of sight.)

Here is a close-up of the chair laying down in order to hammer in the upholstery tacks.

Here's the pretty skirt!

For the cushion, I cut my fabric in a big enough square that the sides of the cushion hung down the four sides at least 3 inches. This includes the height and breadth of the toilet seat itself. I made an envelope by putting some fleece fabric (4 layers) against the wrong sides of the two fabric squares and sewed up three of the four sides. After turning my cushion to the right side I top-stitched the back side that gets tucked under the chair back.

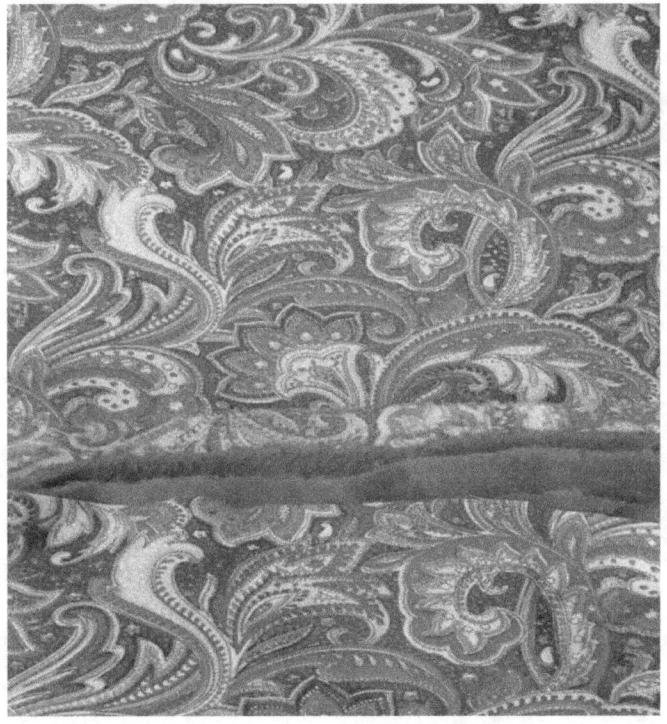

I hand tacked two ribbon ties onto the back of the cushion and tied the cushion to the back of the chair. I could just have easily simply laid the cushion over the toilet seat. As long as the toilet seat is hidden. That's it! Finished!

Ha!  What sits, oh, so, innocently, in a little corner of your cabin is actually your nighttime toilet.  You can stay inside, when the "need" hits you at 2 a.m.

NOTE: To use the toilet, just lift the cushion up against the back of the chair along with the toilet seat back. Here is a "backside picture of my pretty chair toilet (I've pulled the fabric aside):

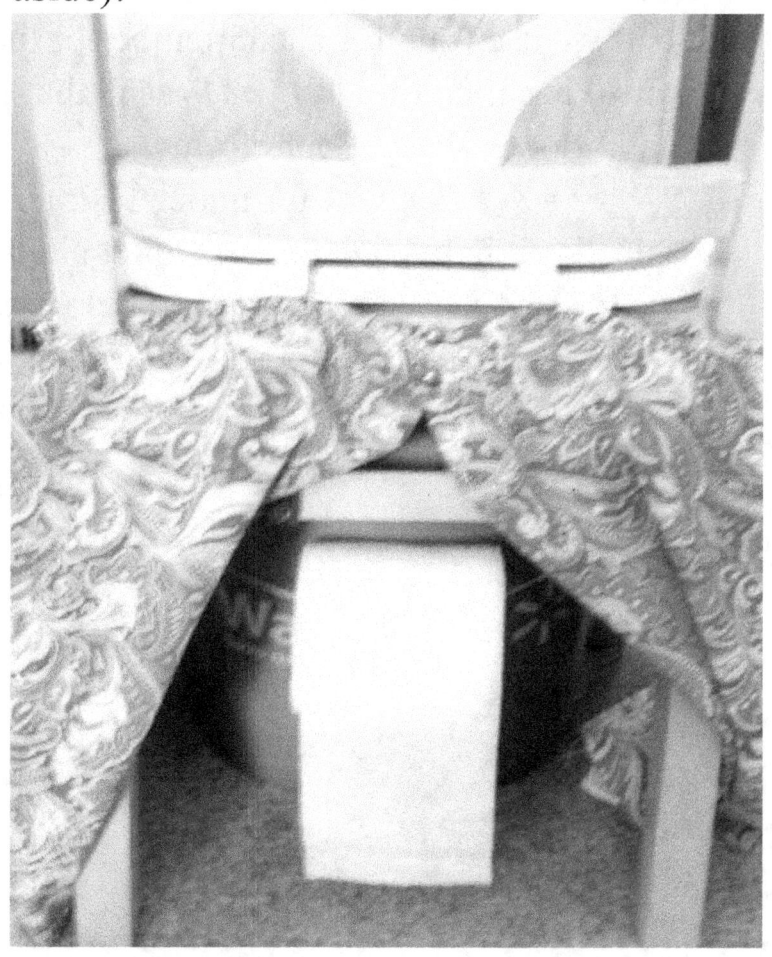

## Toilet Accessory

One more thing before we leave this riveting subject. I highly recommend this wonderful little hygiene item. It's a personal bidet. The brand we use (one for each member of the family) is called the "Proper Wash" that's what it does. We get ours from www.properwash.com for under $10.00. Basically, it helps the, ahem, "toilet sitter" to spray a strong stream of water to help clean the area. In a less than perfect world, at least the private parts, or as Gram used to call them, the "touch me nots", can stay clean.

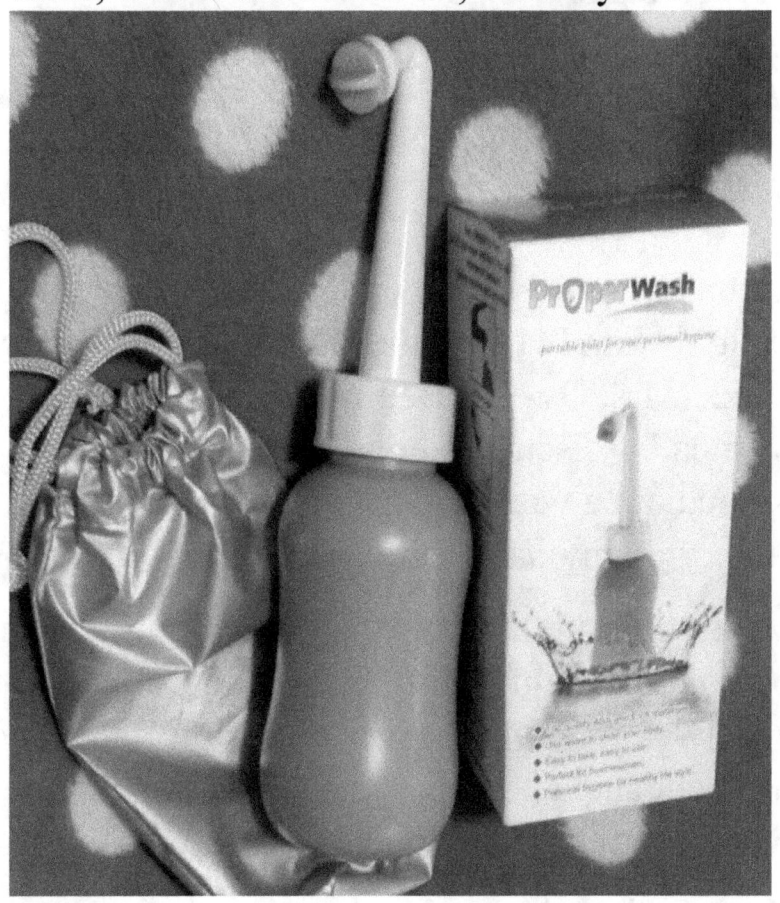

# CHAPTER TWO

## EMERGENCY MEDICINE

Around our house, I'm called "Dr. Mom", but the reality is that I HATE the sight of blood. In my last book, "Mrs. Owen's Beginning Prepper Guide for Women", I discussed how I had not thoroughly washed out a wound in my hand which led to surgery on my hand to remove a tiny bit of gravel.

What I didn't tell you is that, in my cowardly effort to avoid the sight of my own blood, I failed to look closely at my bloody palm. So, triple antibiotic ointment and a bandage caused my hand to "heal" over the little rock.

My point here is that I had to learn to face the stuff I would like to avoid. One way I've done this is to watch a lot of YouTube.com videos made by "Patriot Nurse Channel" and "Dr. Bones and Nurse Amy Channel". I watch until I get used to blood, injuries, diseases, and wounds. It's not fun, but it IS empowering. Empowerment comes from not only planning for the tools needed for emergencies, but being prepared with knowledge of first aid. However, how do you get experience?

An excellent way to get actual experience is with medical training for emergency preparedness. Sign up with your local Red Cross chapter for first aid and CPR (cardio pulmonary resuscitation) classes. (www.redcross.org) In our community these classes are offered on a regular basis and cost under $100. Also, for a fee (about $300) Patriot Nurse travels the country doing excellent day and weekend seminars on all aspects of emergency preparedness medicine. I have not yet attended her seminars, but I watched her you tube videos and she's a kick. I imagine one of the best parts of being at her seminar (or any prepper convention) would be the fun of being around other like-minded folks for a change! (www.thepatriotnurse.com)

## CERT/FEMA.gov Training

There is a blog called "Prepper Chicks" that I follow on Facebook. (www.prepperchicks.org) I love the background image they currently have up on FB. It says, "I am my own FEMA. I'm a prepper". Amen! I want to be my own FEMA. This means that I am not living a mind-set of "in case of an emergency, the government will take care of me."

To this end, Tucker and I will be taking FEMA's CERT training this coming summer. My son-in-law, Hank, the firefighter, told us about it. It's a free and comprehensive training for emergency responders.

CERT stands for Community Emergency Response Teams. As my sweet Hank told me, "Mom, CERT is training private citizens for disaster situations where the 911 operator says, 'We will be there in three or four days.' So prepare now while the information is easy to come by and free." (I love that boy.)

Although this is community training, not wilderness emergency training, I believe there will be a lot of great cross-over information. Check out FEMA.gov and see what they have in your community in the way of CERT training. Here it's a Friday evening, all day Saturday, and all day Sunday. I say it can't hurt. Right?

## Group Medic

We are so blessed to have a nurse in our prepper community. Naturally, she is our assigned group medic. Nurse Bessie keeps a big book that has several pages on each member of our group, including our height, weight, ailments and all medications (with dosages) that we are on. She is also the keeper of the medicine box, although all the adults in our group can access it with her knowledge.

Every prepper group should have at least one designated medic. Of course, having an actual nurse, doctor, or emergency medical technician is a plus, but a rarity, in any prepper group. So, plan to meet this need. Meet it by make sure at least one person, and preferably more than one, get the emergency training needed to care for the medical needs of the individuals in the group.

## CPR

In Book One, I discussed getting antibiotics in your storehouse of preps by purchasing them on eBay.com as fish antibiotics. Antibiotics, clean water, and bandages are a start and will take care of 90% of your medical needs. However, as a dear reader reminded me, triage medicine (prioritizing an individual's or multiple people's medical needs) and emergency medicine MUST be planned for in advance of the problem.

CPR is probably the most valuable prepper medical tool beyond knowing the basics of illness and wound treatment. If someone has a cardiac arrest, it's quite likely his or her life will be saved from the proper use of CPR. According The American Heart Association, 88% of cardiac arrest episodes happen away from the hospital. CPR more than doubles the chances of surviving cardiac arrest. The following is a link to an excellent article if you need any more convincing!

(http://www.heart.org/HEARTORG/CPRAndECC/WhatisCPR/CPRFactsandStats/CPR-Statistics_UCM_307542_Article.jsp )

Our prepper group (the folks we hope will be joining us in an SHTF (stuff hitting the fan) situation) has had a group CPR practice, and we'll be training again next month at our monthly camping weekend.

NOTE: Try to go to your refuge land and camp as often as you can. When we first began to camp as a group, we quickly discovered the holes in our preps. Basically, the things we wish we had at the camp. This can be anything from a pancake turner to an extra pillow.

A great way to learn and practice CPR at home or with a group is to obtain informational diagrams (either free from the internet or purchased as laminated cards from Amazon or other sites.) Here is my favorite free website diagram found at: http://www.funcpr.com/PDFs/CPR%20Diagram.pdf

I have placed American Heart Association charts for giving CPR to adults and to children in the Appendix.

### AED Devices

For the longest time I assumed that defibrillators were just hospital devices. Now I see them everywhere from restaurants to churches. The cost can be as low as $75.00. I have never used one, but my son-in-law, Hank the firefighter, assures me that a voice prompts you within the device and you simply do what it tells you. We now have two of these marvelous and life-saving devices.

## Individual First Aid Kits

We have first aid kits everywhere! I happened into Target one day that they had these cute little red first aid zippered bags on sale for $1.00 apiece. This was about six years ago and they have proved to be so handy. Now, you don't need fancy red bags. A sturdy freezer baggie is one easy solution (at least until you come across some cute bags.)

In each kit I put a minimum of 30 band aids in various sizes, a tube of triple antibiotic ointment (generic Neosporin), sanitary wipes or alcohol wipes (for cleaning the wound area) and pain reliever bottles. I put in the generic equivalent of aspirin, Tylenol, and Advil/Motrin. This is important because some adults with allergies, and most children should not have aspirin. Tylenol is great for general pain and Advil for muscle aches.

## Medicine Chest or Box

This may seem redundant as we've just been putting together our first aid kits, but the medicine chest is its own separate emergency and non-emergency item. The chest (or chests) should be kept locked, if possible. In ours we have our major pain killers (saved over the years from various prescriptions by dentists and doctors,) antibiotics for everything from tooth infections and urinary tract infections to post-operative infection prevention.

NOTE: It is illegal to share prescription medication and it's not recommended you use medication past its expiration date. However, this is a discussion of SHTF/grid down situations where outside medical help is not possible. Use your common sense and stay within the law while there is law to stay within!

The following is a list of what I consider to be the most critical antibiotics to keep in your medicine box: (I will list these in the Appendix along with the common applications/uses and dosages for each.)

1. Fish Flox (Ciprofloxacin)
2. Fish Zole (Metronidazole)
3. Fish Flex (Cephalexin)
4. Fish Mox (Amoxicillin)
5. Fish Forte (Erythromycin.
6. Fish Cycline (Doxycycline)
7. Fish Sulfa and Bird Sulfa (SMZ-TMP)
8. Aquatic Cure (Azithromycin)
9. Fish Cillin (Ampicillin)

For when you are feeling…fishy!

Also consider stocking in your medicine box (besides the basic list I have in Book One) activated charcoal (for tummy problems including food poisoning), tea tree oil, and a good dental kit which would include pain relief gel  Our dental kit was purchased at our local pharmacy for about $12.00.  The kit includes tooth filling material.  Our medicine box does not include a dental extraction kit, but we are planning to add this (and hope we never need it!)

One thing to consider when dealing with deep cuts is in what manner, after cleansing the wound and applying antibiotic ointment, you can sew or otherwise close the wound.  Tucker and I keep a suture kit in our medicine chest that includes sterile suturing needles and sterile thread (about $20.00 on Amazon.)  I also recommend a skin stapler which may, in some cases replace having to sew up a wound.  It's called made by the Oasis Company and costs less than $10.00 for a disposable stapler with 35 sterile staples. A third way to close a wound if it's small enough is butterfly closures, also called Steri Strip closures.  We get ours on Amazon for about $10.00 for 30 three inch strips.

# CHAPTER THREE

## SHOTS

Are you up on your shots?  Most of the young folks I know have been vaccinated, but almost all adults are not current with their boosters.

### Tetanus

Because Tucker and I live on farm, we semi-regularly hurt ourselves (barbed wire, backhoes, pitchforks, you get the picture.)  These accidents mean we are up (reluctantly) on our tetanus shots! But are you?

Tetanus, also known as lockjaw, is a bacteria. Tetanus is not contagious.  It hangs out in the manure of humans and animals.  It also hangs around in the dirt and, as we all know, rusty nails. You get tetanus when a wound gets dirty with tetanus bacteria.

NOTE: Tetanus kills, and before it kills it causes agony to the sufferer.  I'm a great believer in folks being made in the image of God.  Three scientists in France developed the cure.  I don't understand the anti-science movement.  This movement turns its back on hard science which proves vaccinations are safe.

Tetanus vaccines give you protection for up to 10 years. Our doctor recommends every five years. Make sure that this is covered. Dealing with Tetanus in grid down situation would likely be deadly.

### Whooping Cough

Did you know that adults can get vaccinated against whooping cough. Well, I didn't. I began coughing one January and was still coughing in August when we went to the county fair. (I know, I know. I should have gone to the doctor. I just HATE admitting I'm sick. The family is of the opinion that I'll likely die of something preventable. Tucker says I'm the opposite of a hypochondriac.) Anyway, right there at the county fair were our county nurses. A county nurse with a needle in hand, while Tucker and the other nurses pinned me down, gave me a whooping cough shot. Within a week I'd stopped coughing entirely.

### Flu Shots

Flu shots are available every fall and are made up of vaccinations for the most commonly projected flus for that upcoming flu season. Sometimes it doesn't do any good, but most years the shots are life savers. We all get our flu shots each year. The point is laughing at the days to come involves planning for health. Vaccinations are a gift. Science is a good thing; medicine is good. Grow the good sense the Lord gave you!

# CHAPTER FOUR

## FOOD, BEYOND THE BASICS

In Book One, I thought I'd made a fairly exhaustive list of canned goods and other items. However, one my sweet readers pointed out that I'd forgotten dairy. So true. We have dairy goats and chickens. My pea brain assumes everyone else does also!

However, the fact is that even our sweet chickens sometimes choose not to lay (like whenever a fox has been stalking the outside of the henhouse) and our darling Nigerian goats are not always "in milk". (We give them a break towards the end of each birthing season.)

### Eggs

Here is what I've come up with for dairy eggs. We buy "OvaEasy" eggs from the REI online store (www.rei.com). Now, you can buy powdered eggs if you'd like to reminisce about the oh, so wonderful summer camp food you had as a kid, or you can use these amazing egg crystals that cook up like the best scrambled eggs you've ever tasted. I don't know how these folks do it, but they somehow flash freeze and dry the raw eggs so that when you add water it's as if you just cracked them into the mixing bowl.

As of this writing, I pay exactly $5.40 for an envelope of one dozen OvaEasy eggs. The normal price is $6.00 for one envelope. However, only amateurs pay that! After a bit of exploring on the REI site, I found that if I ordered a minimum of 6 dozen (6 envelopes) the price went down to $5.40 per dozen. This is a bit more than eggs at the grocery or Trader Joe's, but not by much. Also, REI ships for free on orders over $50.00 and charges no sales tax. So, I buy these in groups of 10 dozen and pay $54.00. Not a bad way to quickly stock up on eggs in case of a sudden grid down emergency!

NOTE: There eggs are packaged in what look to be Mylar bags. Mylar is one of the best way to keep dry goods fresh. The "best by" date is about two and a half years ahead from my date of purchase, so I figure they are good for at least five years! LOL!

NOTE: I'm not against powdered egg products. I see two problems with them and one advantage. The problems are the taste of powdered eggs (although, I hear that they are just fine as a baking ingredient), and the fact that they seem to only be available in those big #10 cans. A #10 can of powdered eggs is the equivalent of about 13 dozen eggs. Once the can is opened the shelf life drops very quickly. The advantage I see is the longevity of the product (unsealed.) Some brands claim a plus ten year shelf life. The price per dozen breaks down to about the same or somewhat less (depending on the brand) than what I pay for my super yummy OvaEasy eggs.

### Milk

Stock up on cans of evaporated milk, sweetened condensed milk, and powdered milk.

Powdered milk is, surprisingly, the type of milk I've had the most trouble storing. It's as if the milk powder (bought in boxes at the grocery store) comes already stocked with moth larvae! (Not really…) My first attempt at just keeping it in the bags (paper and foil,) that are inside the box, the powdered milk came in did NOT work. After a few months the inside of the sealed (!) bags were crawling with moths and larvae. Gross.

I am now storing our powdered milk in Mylar bags (available on eBay.com) sealed with a hot iron and stored in five gallon buckets. I opened up a bag after storing the dry milk a year ago. The powder remains fresh and unsullied. Yay!

NOTE: When I buy Mylar bags (about a dollar a five gallon bag) I also buy a package of oxygen absorbers and put a 1000cc absorber in each bag on top of whatever dry goods I've poured into the Mylar bag.

### One Bag Meals

I did not invent this kind of all-in-one meal in a bag, but I think I've perfected it!  A one bag meal is an entire one pot dinner that will feed at least 5 people a nourishing and tasty meal.

Making them up is a challenge that I've turned into a game, ok, it's an obsession! The rules are you must fit the entire meal, cans, bottles, bags, and all into a one gallon size freezer bag. The only thing I add to my meals, not in the bag, is water.

NOTE: Did you know that a regular size water bottle is almost exactly two cups? Now you know!

In the Appendix I'll go into detail with my bag ingredients and recipes, but here are a few examples of my one bag meals:

Here is one of the bags with the contents removed:

To make them up I gather all the ingredients for a particular meal, like the above Prepper Ham and Scalloped Potatoes dinner. I make up 10 dinners at a time. Therefore, in assembly line fashion, I line up 10 small canned hams, 10 cans of evaporated milk, 10 envelopes Four Cheese Potato Seasoning,

1 can of peas, and 20 cans of sliced potatoes (each recipe calls for 2 cans of sliced potatoes.)

We (it's a family activity!) each hold a one gallon freezer baggie (because the plastic is thicker than the cheaper storage baggie) and carefully put one entire recipe ingredients into each bags. Then I slide in the recipe card with cooking directions.

All that is needed is a pot, or square pan (depending on the recipe), a fire, and sometimes water.

NOTE: I got these cute recipe cards in the canning aisle. I only write the recipe out once, then I color photocopy it 10 times and slip a copy into each bag.

I've developed nine recipes that the family enjoys. We regularly cook up these meals (after a year in storage) and make up another bag to replace the cooked ingredients. The recipe card goes right back into the bag.

So, nine recipes times ten of each individual dinner gives you 3 months of meals. I figure, if a true SHTF/catastrophic event occurs, I've given myself (and may family) a buffer of 90 days of mindless dinner preparations. I call it a gift to my future self.

# CHAPTER FIVE

## FRUIT TREES

This chapter could have been part of the FOOD…again chapter, but I want to highlight it here because it's really a mind-set. Several years ago Tucker and I agreed that, as much as possible, everything we planted on our property had to give back. This meant instead of maple shade trees, we planted apple trees. Instead of oaks, oranges. See what I mean?

At this point we have cherry, apple, mandarin orange, date, olive, almond, plum, and lemon trees.

For borders we have all kinds of berries. Blueberry, raspberry, blackberry, and boysenberry. I avoid the "thornless" varieties, because deer hate thorns, and I HATE DEER! Why? Only a city girl would ask why.

Well, I was that city girl. Years ago, when Tuck and I first moved to the country, I had a lovely garden, from strawberries and tomatoes, to corn and roses. I even had a small hill dedicated to melons. Watermelons, cantaloupes, muskmelons.

We loved to sit on the porch and watch those elegant deer cross our land. We even bought "deer feed" at our local granary and kept an old wheelbarrow filled for them. Ahhh! The country life. So serene. So peaceful.

Well, around the middle of July, as the crops were getting ready to come in, deer came through one night and literally demolished/ate EVERYTHING. Everything. Decimated. It looked like the land of Egypt after the plagues. I could almost hear the deer bellies grumbling from indigestion.

So thorns are your friends. In fact, if you can use raspberries or some other thorny plant to surround your growing things you are one step ahead. Of course fencing works too, as longs as it high enough that they can't jump it (at least 7 feet.) Another plant group deer hate is lavender and rosemary

Go figure. They'll eat up my sweet roses, thorns and all, (life is full of inconsistencies), but they won't touch lavender and rosemary.

# CHAPTER SIX

## FIRESTARTERS

Firestarters are anything that help to make it easier to get a good fire going. Sometimes this can be as simple as a piece dryer lint and a match. I go through all my day with preparedness on my mind, even if it's just simmering on the back burner.

### Dryer Lint Firestarters

Dryer lint really bothered me for a long time. What could I do with it? Even Martha Stewart had no answers. Then, pyromaniac that I am, I decided to see if it would catch and keep a fire going for any length of time. Well, it caught fire in a nanosecond. However, it went out in about 5 seconds. Sigh.

I ultimately took a look at the internet and found lots of instructions on using this lovely bit of fluff for make longer-lasting Firestarters. For the past couple of years I've been saving dryer lint. As you can imagine, this results in a lot of this lovely stuff!

NOTE: I do a bit of analyzing of the dryer lint before adding it to my lint-saving bag (which is a plastic grocery bag that I keep hanging from a nail next to our washer.) If I've been drying non-cotton items (like a fleece blanket or anything polyester (ewww, not very likely!) then I toss that bit of lint into the regular trash. I don't want a melted bit of plastic mess in any fire I start, especially if it is going into the barbeque or wood stove.

Here's my recipe: (also included in the Appendix, so no need to do anything but read right now.)

Ingredients:

An empty cardboard (not Styrofoam!) egg carton.

A old taper candle (or if you are a candle scrapper, like me, a bunch of used birthday candles)

Dryer lint

To make:

1. Open up your egg carton.
2. Using kitchen shears, cut off the top of the egg carton.
3. Stuff down as much dryer lint into each individual egg cup as will fit.

4. Carefully light a candle (away from the highly flammable lint) DO THIS IN THE SINK!!
5. Holding the candle at an angle, drip wax into each egg cup on top of the lint until the melted wax soaks into the lint and begins to cover it. (about 25 drops of wax from the candle)
6. Let the egg carton get cool and dry. Just walk away for a few minutes.
7. Carefully tear or cut each egg cup away until you have a dozen free little Firestarters!

Stuff

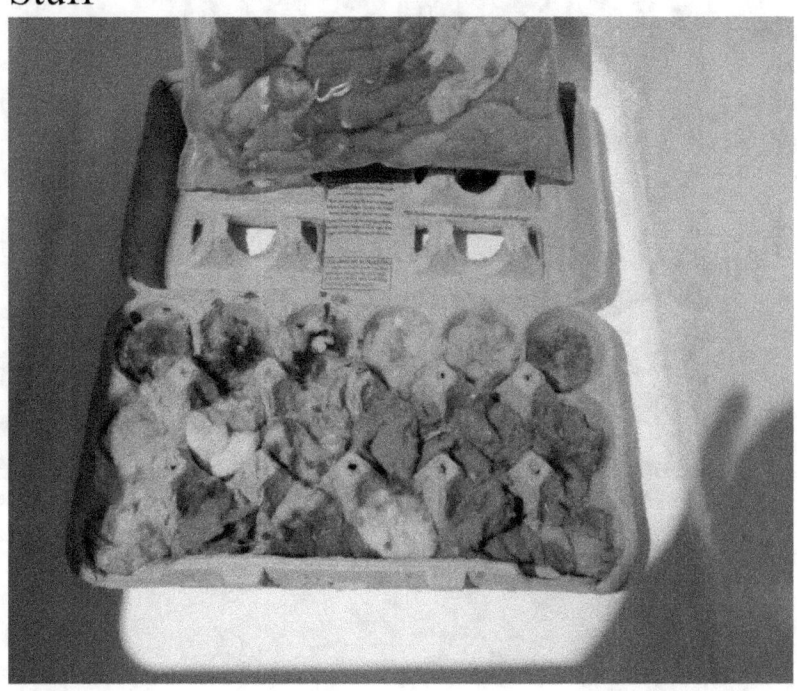

Melt

## Cut and Store!

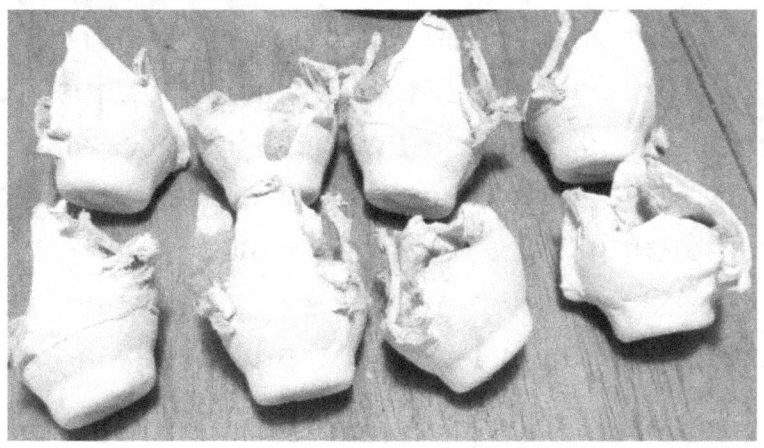

These little Firestarters will ignite easily with a flint or a match and can be used to start wood fires in your wood stove or campfire. They will burn at least 5 minutes with a very strong flame. More than long enough to get a fire going!

You will have the other half of the egg carton left over. I'm still workin' on what to do with that. For now it goes into the recycle box, which just about kills me. If you come up with a use for these bits of cardboard, email me at mrstuckerowen@hotmail.com or write to me on Facebook at KATIE OWEN!

NOTE: Do not save junk, such as the unused half of the egg carton. If you start saving every scrap you will become a "hoarder", instead of a prepper. Only save what is on your emergency preparedness list. Of course, this list can be added to, just keep things tidy. Also, don't gather 10 grocery bags full of dryer lint and 100 cardboard egg cartons and stack them in your garage. Be disciplined. Make up these Firestarters whenever you have enough materials to make 1-4 dozen individual starters.

## Cotton Ball Firestarters

This firestarter is so easy! Go to the dollar store and buy a big container of petroleum jelly (brand name: Vaseline) and a couple of bags of cotton balls. Just store them together in a gallon size plastic bag or a shoe box labelled Fire! All you have to do is dip a cotton ball into the petroleum jelly (a dap will do). A flint or a match will make a fire. Just put the soaked ball at the bottom of your kindling pile and set it on fire. Whoosh! Instant fire!

## Cosmetic Pads Firestarter

I buy makeup remover pads at the dollar store. You know those round or square all cotton things? They sell them in bags of 80-150 (depending on the shape) for a dollar. Each on makes one or two

Firestarters, so they calculate out to a penny or so a piece. I use them the same way as the egg cup and cotton ball Firestarters. The nice thing about the cosmetic pad Firestarters is that the light even easier (if that's possible) than the other two. Once made, I tear one in half and all these little cotton fibers are exposed, just beggin' to be set fire.

Here's how I make them:

Only two ingredients: a cotton pad and wax. Those two ingredients, wax or parchment paper and a pot are all you need.

NOTE: I have a dedicated pan for melting wax because it's just too hard to clean out wax in a pot once it has been used to melt wax.

1. I take a quarter of a wax block (available at all craft stores and eBay and Amazon) and melt it slowly (keep your stove on the lowest setting.)
2. Take the pot off the stove and dip one half of the pad, then the other half until its covered in wax.

3. Lay each pad down on some wax paper and let cool.
   Then bag them in sandwich size bags (about 10 per baggie.)

You can easily make 100 in about thirty minutes.

NOTE: To catch the pads on fire, just tear on in half. You will see little cotton fibers where the tear was made. Light the fibers (don't hold the pad when lighting!) and place your kindling over the flame. Fire!

NOTE: You know those big red plastic rectangular tubs with lids that the big box stores (like Wal-Mart and K-Mart) sell at Christmas? I have a big one that is clearly labelled "FIRE!" on all sides and the top using black permanent marker. In it I store all my Firestarters, along with flints, matches, and BBQ lighters. It's very easy to spot when fire is needed quick.

# CHAPTER SEVEN

## ROOT CELLARS / COLD STORAGE

In Book One my intent is to encourage beginning preppers to start gathering food, water, and supplies. Getting started is often the hardest part of prepping. In Book One I did not spend much time discussing the storage of these items.

As any dedicated prepper knows, finding storage is a challenge to say the least. At this point, most of our preps are stored on our refuge land, but certainly not all.

NOTE: We live in a warm climate, so keeping the food at a cool enough temperature is my biggest challenge. If you are blessed to have a basement that's the greatest place to store food

Years ago, as our pantry filled up, I hid cans and jars under all the beds, then behind the couches (hidden against the wall), in the closets and finally, and reluctantly, in the garage (which heats up in spring and summer). We have no basement due to flooding in our area. Finally, we had run out of room.

Also, we became more and more concerned that when the big SHTF day came along (ya, know, the Get.Out.Now.Day in Matthew 24) we'd be hurtin'. Why? Because, ALL our preps were at our house a good twenty miles from our refuge. Even assuming we had transportation, it would take several days of driving back and forth to move it all.

Tucker, bless his heart, worked it out…

### Shipping Containers

Proper food storage of any type of food, commercial canned, pressure canned, dry goods in buckets, and purchased dried and canned foods, can last 20+ years if stored in a cool environment. A huge refrigerator, freezer and an air conditioned house will take care of this problem! Um, no. Solving the problem of food storage off grid (ie: no electricity, hot summers, etc.) is a pickle. There is not easy way, but we've found a few solutions that I hope will inspire you.

Tucker's pride and joy is his backhoe.  Don't be found callin' it a tractor, he'll instantly correct you. (and by you, I mean <u>me</u>.)

He went to work with the backhoe and cut into one of our little hills a perfect rectangle, sides flaring out to avoid a cave-in, with slight downhill drainage.  Then he bought two 20 foot shipping containers that he slid right in.  (Actually, the container delivery guys slid them right in.)

The containers are insulated by having three sides up against the soil.  The fourth side he fronted with cement block (accept for a door opening for each). The roof he covered in several layers of insulation (that pink stuff) and then a large tarp. Then he built a wood deck on the top.

He did not want to put soil (which is crazy heavy as it turns out) on the roof.  He wants there to be no danger of cave-ins.

Now we have quite a bit of "root cellar" type storage that stays cool (between 50-60 degrees) year round.

Here are the storage containers before the dirt was backfilled around the sides, the insulated roof deck put on, and the fronts faced with concrete block.

Of course, a root cellar can be dug into the ground if you don't have any hills. A cellar dug down at least six feet (the deeper it is the easier to move around and stand up). Then, keeping the floor dirt, add a "footing of concrete around all three sides. We do this slowly so that we can place concrete blocks on the wet cement as we go around the cellar. The concrete blocks are placed up against each other. At the corners we chip at the block until it fits snuggly against the one next to it. Tucker, is always afraid of cave-in and stands 2-3 foot rebar up inside each block as we work around the room. Once you have one layer of cement footing and concrete block, add the next one. Be sure to stagger the blocks so that the bricks are not lined up one after the other. Take a look at any brick wall and you'll see what I mean. Once he has two rows completed, Tucker pours concrete down the holes in the center of the blocks which make the wall solid and grabs the rebar inside. Keep this up (pouring concrete and rebar every two rows up) until you've reached the top. Once you are at ground level you can either top it with an insulated deck (like our shipping container tops) or add plywood across the top and adding strong lumber (like 2x6's) build a floor for a cabin built above it.

We will be building this root cellar/basement in our next tiny house and plan to put a trap door into the floor with a ladder going down to reach our food storage. This next cabin is my dream cabin. Tucker and I will be writing about our tiny house adventures in Book Three.

## Refrigerators and Freezers

No, I'm not suggesting you plug in refrigerator and freezer! I'm suggesting you give them a decent burial! Seriously, both appliances are well insulated and burying them face up into the soil makes for dandy cold storage. Dig a hole in the ground just wide and long and deep enough to drop the appliance down into the ground. Leave the door/s uncovered and you take out all the shelves (which are now really just dividing the inside space.)

## Trash Cans and Ice Chests

This is the same idea as the larger appliances. Just drop them in the ground for smaller cold storage. A metal trash can in the ground would be ideal place to store medicines that need to be kept cool and dark.

# CHAPTER EIGHT

## REFUGE LAND

Where do you live? If you are in the city, you may have already lost the battle before it begins. I know that's harsh, but how serious are you that we are entering into a SHTF time? In a real, long-term, emergency getting out of a city, especially with little ones, will put you into grave danger.

Transportation may be limited or non-existent. Do not assume you can just pack up your car and drive away. EVERYONE in your city will have the same idea. Some of those folks will not think twice about taking what you have. The nicer folks will still be contributing to traffic jams, grocery store food runs, and gas lines. Those kinder folks quickly drop the niceness if their own and/or their family's lives are at stake. So, work now, at getting rural.

If you can't live in a rural environment right away, start planning to purchase a large piece of land that you will go to AHEAD of the crowds. Getting ahead of the rabble requires vigilant watching of the world around you. Be diligent. In my opinion, we are almost there, but I'm conscientiously tuning to FOX news and checking out our local news internet site. Local, national, and international news will keep you apprised fairly well.

NOTE: I may be a bit overboard on this, but I keep the news on the T.V. all day. I mute the sound, but look over regularly to see what's happening. I love that scrolling news thing at the bottom of the screen.

Now, to finding your perfect land: Imagine the desperate hordes of folks fleeing the city closest to you. Say, an EMP solar blast has taken out the electricity nationwide. Very shortly, folks will leave the waterless and foodless municipality to richer "pastures".

Don't let that richer pasture be yours. Before choosing our ideal land, Tucker and I poured over maps of our area for about 150 miles around. We knew we wanted land that would be off the beaten path (literally). The kind of land that walking or driving out-of-towners would never even notice.

That means a road (preferably) dirt that was off a road… that was off a road… that was off a main highway.  Get the idea?

We began looking at real estate advertisements for "rural land".  We never looked at any land with a house on it.  We did not look at land with electricity running to it.  We preferred dirt roads. Finally, we found our land which is many acres off a road that is off a road…you understand.  The best part is the "NO OUTLET" sign at the initial turnoff about 3 miles from our land.

The added advantage is that this truly "off grid" land tends to be the cheapest around!  The closer you get to civilization the higher the prices for land go.  Weird, huh?  This is due to a desire for convenience over safety.

We started with one little "cottage" on our land and now, including the cabins built by the members of our refuge group, we have eleven.  No electricity (we don't want lines leading the hoards to our property) will likely ever be part of our refuge land.

# CHAPTER NINE

## WELLS AND STREAMS

### Wells

Once you get your land you will need to focus on your group's water needs. We bought our land raw as a newborn baby. It had no well and just a seasonal stream. However, we saved up and had a well put in by professionals at a cost of $9,000.00. Since then we've learned how to drill wells ourselves.

Our inspiration came from http://www.howtodrillawell.com/ . Wells are not new. Pioneers have been hand-digging them for millennia. The kit we bought is a heck of a lot easier than hand-digging and thousands of dollars cheaper than using a professional well-driller. It's still not cheap, however. Our kit plus the rental of a large air compressor cost about $600.

Our hope is that as our group work together, we will have a well for each cabin on our refuge land. We are treating each well like a community barn-raising. (We've done the same with some of the cabins.) Unlimited water should be the goal of every prepper.

## Streams

Our refuge land has a seasonal stream. When it runs it gives us lots of water. After buying our land, the first thing we did was figure out how to reap and store some of the water for ourselves.

A few years ago Tucker followed the stream uphill from our camp until he came across a modest waterfall (about six feet high). Then, he got a large animal trough (black rubber kind) and drilled a hole in the bottom front. He added fittings over the hole so that a garden hose could screw into the fittings.

NOTE: We buy industrial type water hoses. Ours are a brownish red. The rubber is thicker and is of a material that won't degrade so quickly in outdoor environments.

Then he placed the trough (with some heavy boulders inside it to keep it in place) under the falling water. As the running water filled and overfilled the trough, the hose also filled with water which ran downstream and into our 2500 gallon water tank. Over the years we've added interconnecting 2500 -3000 gallon tanks (each a bit downhill from each other) and they fill as the one above reaches capacity and overflows into another garden hose.

We do our best each year to keep these filled with the stream water as our well water must be hand-pumped out. Someday, we'll look into solar well pumps.

# CHAPTER TEN

## WHO IS IN YOUR GROUP?
## (AND HOW TO PICK EM')

As the writer of Hebrews said, *"Not forsaking the assembling of ourselves together, as the manner of some is; but exhorting one another: and so much the more, as you see the day approaching." –* Hebrews 10:25

"Not forsaking the assembly of ourselves" means there are strength in numbers. Different people, different skills, stronger group.

I know of good and honorable folks who plan to ride a SHTF on their own. Why? Different reasons. Some people just don't "play well with others". However, I think that most of these "loners" want a group of like-minded people, they just don't know where to start.

I'll be the first to admit that forming a group is extremely difficult. So many things factor into your choice of members. For Tucker and me, the most important thing is to have a group of real Christians.

NOTE:  For years, we've used the term "have a nice day" (HAND) churches.  That's the folks who seem to have formed a type of country club, rather than a real church formed around Jesus Christ.  The HAND church members don't seem to have any sense of something beyond themselves.  The focus seems to be on numbers, dollars, and church building programs.  (I'm allergic to church building programs!)

Real Christians know they are miserable sinners in need of the Savior.  Mature Christians are also aware of the world around and are comparing prophecy to the news on T.V.  That means that they grieve for the lost and pray for the persecuted, seeing persecution happening worldwide against Christians.  They are aware the world is spiraling down and are making plans to hide when the persecution reaches our country.

Tucker and I are believers who do not subscribe to the "pretribulation rapture" theory so rampant in the HAND churches.  This "Jesus will take us out of here before the poor suckers "left behind" will experience tribulation" thinking is dangerous and false.  Jesus is VERY clear in Matthew 24 (and elsewhere in Scripture) that Christians are going to suffer through a time that will be worse than anything experienced in the history of the world. At the end of it He will return.

NOTE: LOL, if I have not lost you at this point, let me tell you that I am writing a Mrs. Owen's Devotional Guide for Women Preppers. So, stay tuned!

So, back to how to pick your group. For us prayer is key. Putting legs to our prayers, Tucker and I very carefully over the years have introduced the topic of preparedness to many folks, mostly friends from church, and noted their reactions and thoughts on the subject. Keep in mind that you could be trusting the folks in your refuge group with your lives. So, move slowly in this area and DO NOT give out too much information about your preps.

In our case, we invite people we think might be candidates up to our refuge land for a picnic. Ya know, just a time of eating, hiking, and ATV riding. This knocks out a bunch of candidates right away, because many people don't seem too interested in nature and hiking. That's ok. We just need information and if you are turned down, that's excellent data to store away.

We also look for folks who like to build or camp. We look for skills, basically and a desire to live more simply. That's not to say the luxury vacation types won't eventually come around. I'm amazed at the folks in our group and where they've come from. We've got a nurse, a child psychologist, a firefighter, a chef, an electrical lineman, Sally and Dave, a retired missionary couple (boy do they know how to rough it!), a building contractor, four homeschool moms, many, many children (enough for a one-room schoolhouse!), a retired Navy chaplain, and even a couple of lawyers. (Still trying to figure out their 'skills', lol—not really!)

Together we've cleared land, built cabins, collected food and supplies, learned pressure canning, studied first aid, developed a shooting range and practiced with our guns, and a zillion other things. We also fellowship together, with our Chaplain leading us. We enjoy each other's company more and more as we work and camp together.

Obviously, finding like-minded folks is very personal and totally individual to each group. But basically all the members have to share the same moral values and future goals in common. The healthy adults know that they are expected to pull their own weight.

Our diverse group came together gradually and "organically" over time. I tried to push it, but found it's not possible.

Nevertheless, I believe we did not form our group, the Lord did!. Tucker and I are pretty sure others will show up with nothing. We will help them as much as we are able.

# CHAPTER ELEVEN

## HOMESCHOOL

My older children were public-school educated. My younger children were homeschooled. For those able to be at home to homeschool, I can tell you there is no comparison. Homeschooled kids consistently perform better on standardized tests (like SATs) than public school educated children.

However, this is not why I love it. To be quite honest, I just love being with my kids all day. I'm not that parent who dreaded summer vacation when the kids were released from school for the summer break. I'm the parent who grew sad as September approached and I knew we'd see less of each other. When they finally arrived home at the end of the school day, they were too worn out to want to do something fun (like cooking sewing, gardening, etc.)

I love my kids. Tucker and I would rather be with them all the time. Tucker says we are like the farm families from years gone by when the entire family was in close proximity to one another all day.

In any case, whether or not you homeschool at this time, consider preparing to do so in a grid down/SHTF time. Do you have or anticipate you'll have little ones in your refuge group? Little minds need to be occupied and learning. Plan now.

Now I'm not suggesting trigonometry or astrophysics (unless you love these subjects!) books. I am simply suggesting good literature (I covered this somewhat in Book One) and plenty of writing tablets and pens and pencils. Basic math can be taught without any books, but there are some great elementary math workbooks that are not expensive. I love the Horizons series (available on Amazon for about $15.00 plus another (used) teacher answer book for $5.00.

I've tried a lot (a. lot.) of different curriculum companies touted by my homeschool friends. What I've found with literally all of the curriculum companies, is that the amount of subjects, reading, and assignments are WAY too much. One simply cannot get through all the material. (The companies always say that all the material does not need to be used, but it's in tiny print.)

This curriculum deluge sets up the homeschooling mom for failure. I have a theory. I believe the companies do this is to prove their superiority to other company's curriculum, or heaven forbid, the parent's own curriculum they put together for themselves.

For several years now I choose my child's study by taking a look at the suggested reading for each grade level (available by doing an Amazon search or looking at the tiny pictures of the books included in the curriculum company's literature for that grade level) and then I order those reading books, plus any other book I want them to read, from Amazon's used books. Cost is about $20.00-$30.00 per grade. On top of reading, we study the Bible together, write stories, do book reports, etc.

A great book series to use now to quietly help your children learn skills for SHTF days is the Little House on the Prairie series of books by Laura Ingalls Wilder. With this series I purchase the Little House Primer. Over the course of the year we learned about and practiced everything from making Johnny Cakes to tanning animal skins.

In addition to actual books, workbooks, paper and pencils, plan to have plenty of outdoor lessons in a grid down homeschool. Think now about nature walks to learn about beneficial and poisonous plants, building, using hammers and nails, outdoor cooking, including fire building and fire safety, star-gazing (a basic book on constellations and planets would be great!), animal husbandry, and beekeeping. (As a beekeeper, I keep some littler beesuits just for this purpose.)

# CONCLUSION

## THE ULTIMATE PREP

No matter how long and hard you prepare for all contingencies, there is one prep you can't make on your own…

Sometimes it seems to me that folks forget that we are all gonna die. So many diets and wrinkle creams (to "diminish signs of aging"), and cosmetic surgery, cater to the LIE that if you do this or that you'll never die. We humans know we are on a fixed schedule for death, but we are very, very, good at avoiding this reality.

*"it is appointed unto men once to die, but after this the judgment." Hebrews 9:27*

According to the book of Revelation there are two deaths. The first death we all go through. The second is the judgment. According to John in Revelation 20:6:

*"Blessed and holy is he that hath part in the first resurrection: on such the second death hath no power,"*

Scripture is clear. Those who are "blessed and holy" have no part in the second death.

So how does one become blessed and holy? I don't know about you, but I have sinned so many times I've lost count. Just take a look at the Ten Commandments. How many have you kept? Me? I think I've broken them all either physically or in my heart.

Paul, the apostle says, *"For all have sinned and fallen short of the glory of God." Roman 3:23.*

Solomon wrote, *"For there is not a just man upon earth, that doeth good, and sinneth not." Ecclesiastes 7:20*

So, the first step in the ultimate prep is to admit your sin. You (and me, too!) are a sinner.

That's right. You can't make yourself holy no matter how hard you try. Our good works, according to the prophet Isaiah,

*"are as **filthy rags"** Isaiah 64:6*

So what to do? We can't save ourselves. Billy Graham can't even save himself (and he'd be the first to admit this.) What happens if we die in our sin, unholy, not blessed? Death. Not physical death. That happens to everyone, the holy and blessed and the unsaved. It's the second death that comes from dying in sin.

*""For the wages of sin is death; but the gift of God is eternal life through Jesus Christ our Lord." Romans 6:23*

Did you see that last part? There is hope!! This is the hope that sends me laughing at the days to come!

*"For God so loved the world that He gave His only begotten Son, that whoever believes in Him SHALL NOT PERISH, but have everlasting life." John 3:16*

What does that mean, "He sent His Son?"

*""But God demonstrates His own love toward us, in that while we were still sinners, Christ died for us." Romans 5:8*

Good news! Jesus, God's Son, died for you. He took the punishment you deserve for your sin on

Himself at the cross. He died for you. He died for me. Just typing these words fills me with awe.

My kids are always calling something awesome, knowing I'm gonna say, "Only God is awesome." It's true. Only God is awesome.

Jesus died for you on the cross to take away your sins and make you …BLESSED AND HOLY! Yay! Hallelujah!!

He did not stay dead. He couldn't. He is God. On the third day after His crucifixion, He rose from the dead.

So, what's step two in the ultimate prep?

*"if you confess with your mouth Jesus as Lord, and believe in your heart that God raised Him from the dead, you will be saved: for with the heart a person believes, resulting in righteousness, and with the mouth he confesses, resulting in salvation." "for everyone who calls on the name of the Lord will be saved." Romans 10:9-10,13*

That's it. Admit your sin. Confess with your mouth that Jesus is Lord and died for you. Believe in your heart that God raised Him from the dead. AND YOU WILL BE SAVED.

That's the ultimate prep. If you want to talk, shoot me an email at mrstuckerowen@hotmail.com.

# APPENDIX

## CHAPTER ONE – TOILETS IN DISGUISE

### How to Make a Pretty Chair Toilet

Here's my step by step of the process. I'll include all of this information and the pictures again in the Appendix. No need to take notes. I've done it for you. Here are the "ingredients":

1. Find wooden chair that will make a good candidate for a toilet. (That sentence looks funny even to me!)

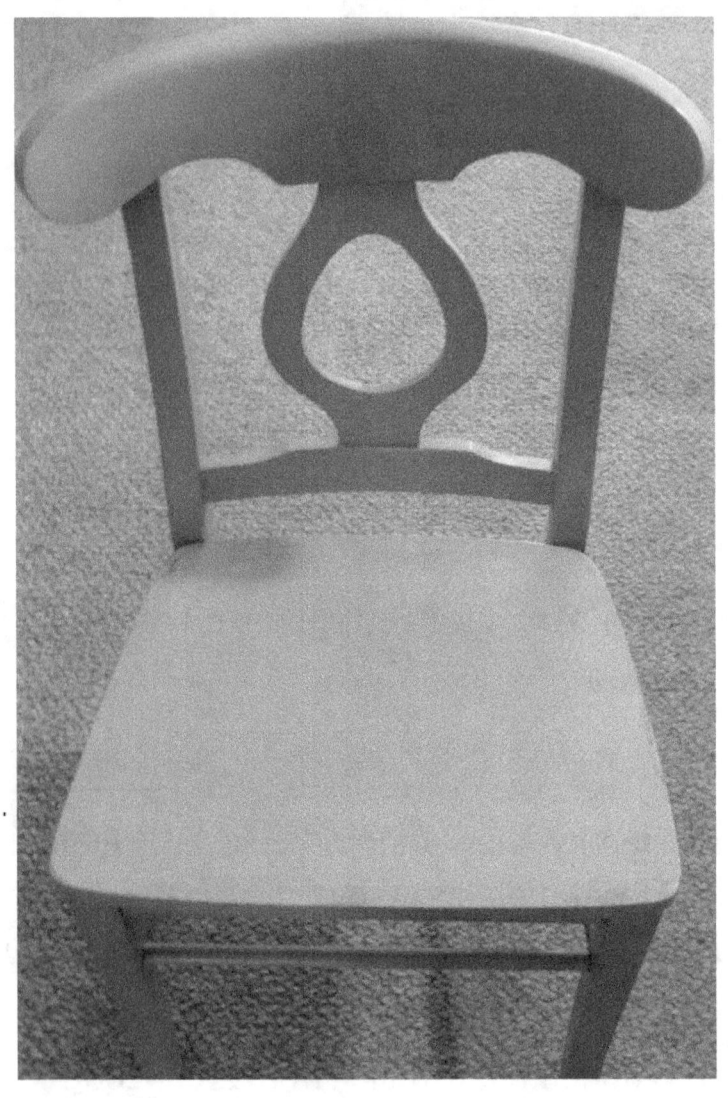

A "good candidate" is one whose seat height is at least 15 inches from the floor to the bottom of the seat. The height should not be more than 20 inches or the "waste" will have to drop a bit too far down.  Also, the chair seat itself must be at least 13 inches round, square, or rectangle.  In other words, make sure that if the seat is removed you can drop a five gallon bucket down the middle of it without the bucket getting stuck. (LOL, as I write this, I'm sitting in Starbucks eying their "good candidate" chairs and plotting my next toilet!)


NOTE: I've given this a lot of thought and you can use furniture items other than chairs.  How about a side table whose dimensions fit the "good candidate" above?  Or even a stool.  Granted the stool would need to be short and wide, but I've seen them.  Shop the thrift stores.  You'll find lots of candidates.

Our side table would be a great candidate:

2.  A five gallon bucket (sold at all hardware stores and Wal-Mart for a few dollars. (No swim noodle is needed for the chair toilet)
3. A toilet seat.  Be sure to get the "standard" size, not the fancy elongated kind. I paid $5.00 at Wal-Mart
4. Three yards of any fabric you think is pretty.
5. Stuffing, quilt batting, or a fleece throw (Again, about $5.00 at Wal-Mart) for the cushion.  This cushion, made with the same fabric or a contrasting fabric, will be the last thing you make to lay over the toilet seat and thus, disguise the true function of your chair.
6. Two bungee cords.
7. A package of elastic
8. Upholstery nails (also known as decorative nails or thumbtacks)
9. A sewing machine or a sewing needle with thread.

This chair toilet takes about 2 hours start to finish. Take a look at the step by step pictures I've provided and you will see how fun it was.

To Begin:

1. Take off the seat of your chair. Most chair seats are simply screwed in place under the seat.

2. Place the entire toilet seat and top on the chair base.

Note: Depending on the opening, you may need to fasten some wood strips in place to make the opening smaller. If you are working with a side table you will need to draw an opening on the top (the same size as the opening in your toilet seat) and use a jig saw to cut the opening.

3. Now attach your toilet seat to the back of your chair using bungee cords.

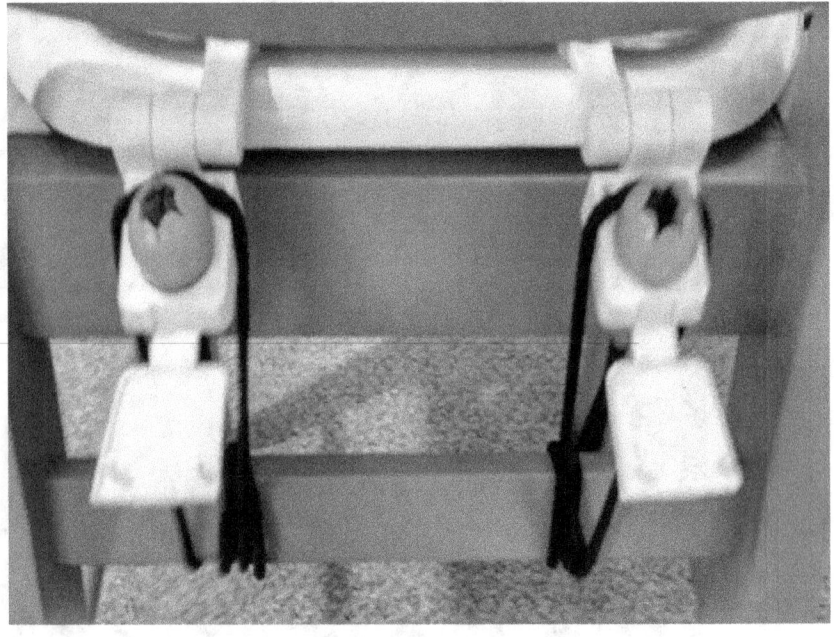

That's it, except for placing the bucket (that has an inch or more of sawdust or kitty litter inside the bottom) on the floor under the chair!  Now comes the fun part!  The decorating! Yep! We Proverbs 31 women preppers love to embellish!

The first chair I got was already painted a pretty green, so I did not paint it. However, that would be the next step if the color or finish is not to your liking.

First thing I did was cut my fabric lengthwise (I just ripped down the middle of all three yards), then holding the fabric against the chair seat area I pinned down, then ironed, the raw edge on the top (about an inch for my chair) so that I had a clean, folded edge at the top.  I made the fabric length just long enough to puddle a bit on the floor and just wide enough (about 1 ½ times to go around the entire circumference of the chair).  I did this to give it a full, country-gathered look.  I then measured the elastic to the measurement of the circumference of the seat area and took off about three inches to give it some stretch.

NOTE: If my instructions sound hazy, just take a look at the pictures. Hopefully, the pictures will make the "how to" crystal clear.

Using my sewing machine, I folded the two short ends of the skirt and sewed down the fold to hide any raw edges. The, using a lot of pins, I zigzagged the stretched elastic around the inner (wrong side) edge.

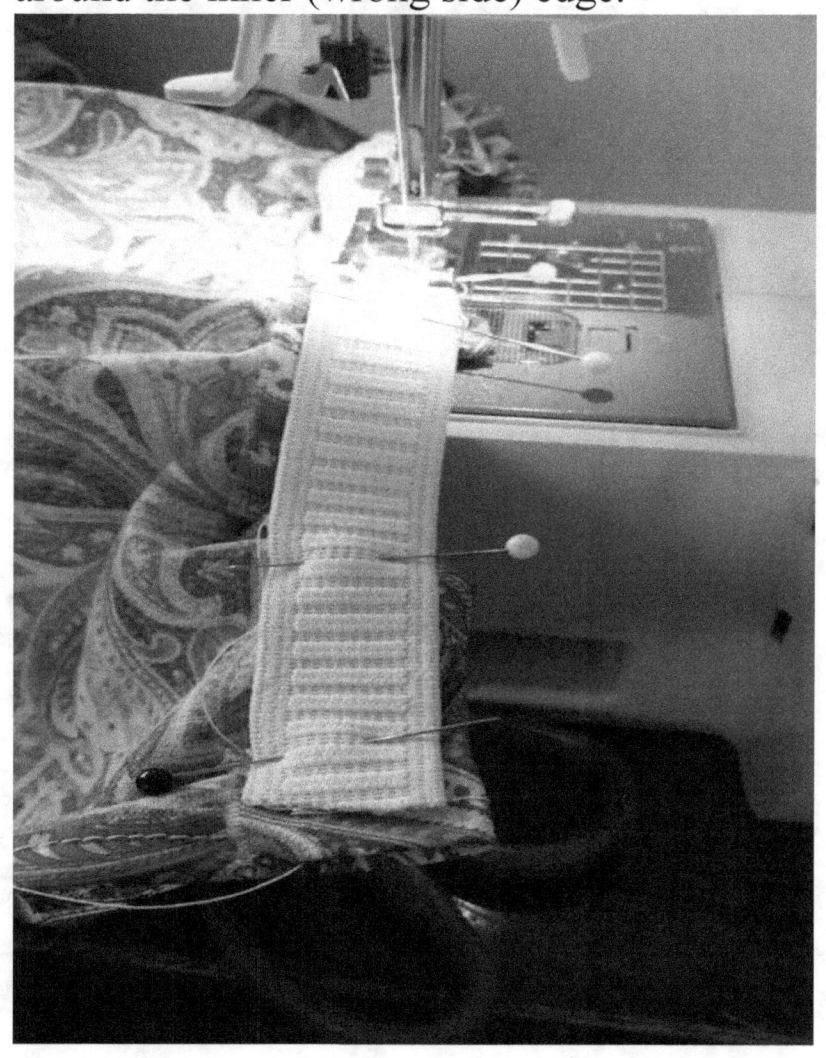

Once you've sewed the elastic to the skirt it is done!

Now take those tacks and little hammer and beginning at the back, tack the skirt onto the outer edge of the chair seat area. I started with two tacks in the back where the two folded over edges meet. (This is the flap opening to access your bucket.) We also use the bucket handle to hold the toilet paper out of sight.)

Here is a close-up of the chair laying down in order to hammer in the upholstery tacks.

That's the skirt!

For the cushion, I cut my fabric in a big enough square that the sides of the cushion hung down the four sides at least 3 inches. This includes the height and breadth of the toilet seat itself. I made an envelope by putting some fleece fabric (4 layers) against the wrong sides of the two fabric squares and sewed up three of the four sides. After turning my cushion to the right side I top-stitched the back side that gets tucked under the chair back.

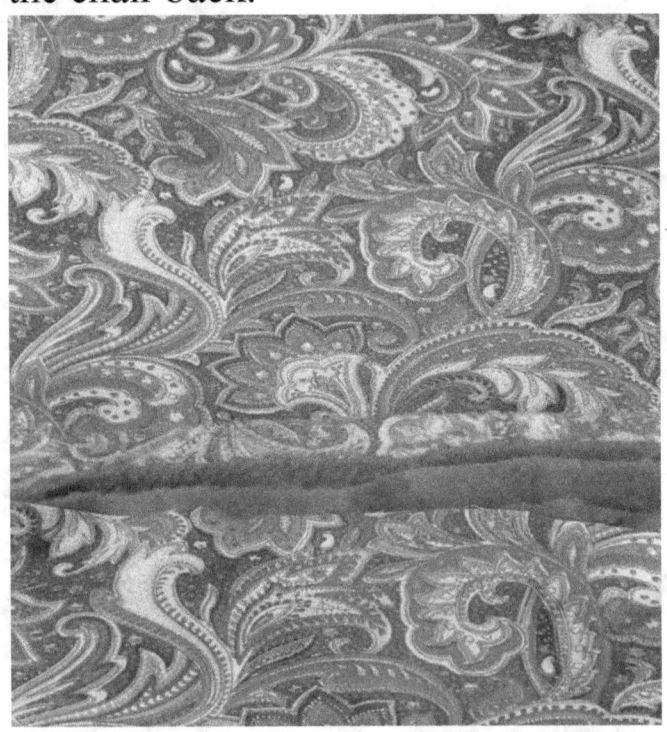

I hand sewed two ribbon ties onto the back of the cushion and tied the cushion to the back of the chair. I could just have easily simply laid the cushion over the toilet seat. As long as the toilet seat is hidden. That's it! Finished!

NOTE: To use the toilet, just lift the cushion up against the back of the chair along with the toilet seat back.

Here is a "backside picture of my pretty chair toilet (I've pulled the fabric aside):

 Finally, I highly recommend this wonderful little hygiene item.  It's a personal bidet.  The brand we use (one for each member of the family) is called the "Proper Wash" that's what it does.  We get ours from www.properwash.com for under $10.00.

# CHAPTER TWO - EMERGENCY MEDICINE

**NOTE: You MUST do your own research before taking any of these medications. Some folks are allergic to some types of antibiotics. Some antibiotics pass through breast milk. Some are DANGEROUS for pregnant women, nursing mothers, and children. This is NOT medical advice! The information below is a collation of my research from discussing these meds with our doctors, internet research, listening to Patriot Nurse's and other's youtube.com talks, and from Dr. Vince, a medical doctor in Washington State who advises our family. (www.antibioticsforsurvival.com)**

1. Fish Flox (Ciprofloxacin)

Dosage: 500mg. every 12 hours for 10 days.

Cipro is best for UTI (urinary tract infections,) bladder infections, bronchitis, pneumonia, anthrax, and bacterial infections of the intestinal tract. <u>It is not safe for pregnant or nursing women, or for children.</u>

2. Fish Zole (Metronidazole)

Dosage: 250 – 500 mg every 8 hours for 10 days.

Treats intestinal bacteria and diverticulitis and skin infections. <u>It is not safe for pregnant or nursing women, or for children</u>

3. Fish Flex (Cephalexin)

Dosage: 250 mg every 6 hours for 7-14 days.

Will treat almost any any type of respiratory infection (pneumonia, strep, bronchitis, etc.) and ear infections. <u>It is safe for pregnant women and children</u>

4. Fish Mox (Amoxicillin)

Dosage: 500 mg every 12 hours for 10 days.

Sinus and ear infections, strep throat, and the same types of bacteria as Cephalexin. <u>It is unknown whether it is safe for pregnant and nursing mothers and children to take this.</u>

5. Fish Forte (Erythromycin)

Dosage: 250-500 mg every 6 hours for 10 days.

Kills the same types of bacteria as Cephalexin. <u>It's also safe for pregnant women and children</u>.

6. Fish Cycline (Doxycycline)

Dosage: 100 mg every 12 hours for the first day (24 hours), then 100 mg. every day for 7 10 days.

Treats illness due to tick bites. Treats the same types of infections as Erythromycin. It also treat sinus infections, Typhus and Malaria. <u>It should not be used by children, pregnant women or nursing mothers.</u>

7. Fish Sulfa and Bird Sulfa (SMZ-TMP)

Dosage: One tablet every 12 hours for 10-14 days for UTI and bronchitis.

Short for Sulfamethoxazole and Trimethoprim. This can treat most respiratory infections, but it is most commonly used for urinary tract infections. Probably the most critical need for this antibiotic is that it can treat MRSA (Methicillin-resistant Staphylococcus aureus), also known as "resistant staph." This is a type of bacteria that is resistant to most antibiotics. <u>Not safe for pregnant or nursing mothers, elderly, or young children.</u>

8. Aquatic Cure (Azithromycin)

Dosage: 500 mg on day one. 250 mg per day for four days.

Treats all respiratory infections, Chlamydia, Lyme disease, PID, Syphilis, and Typhoid. <u>Probably safe for pregnant and nursing mothers. Not recommended for infants.</u>

9. Fish Cillin (Ampicillin)

Dosage: 250 – 500 mg every 6 hours for 10 days.

This a broad-spectrum type of penicillin, but Ampicillin is more effective against anthrax. Also treats respiratory infections, meningitis, urinary tract infections, and gastrointestinal infections. <u>Safe for pregnant women.  Unsafe for nursing mothers or young children.</u>

# Heartsaver®
## Adult CPR AED

American
**Heart**
Association®
*Learn and Live*

Tap and shout

Yell for help. Send someone
to phone 911 and get an AED

Look for no breathing or
only gasping

Push hard and fast.
Give 30 compressions

 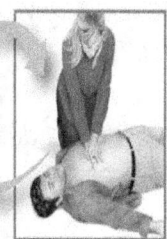

Open the airway and give
2 breaths

Repeat sets of 30 compressions
and 2 breaths

When the AED arrives, turn it
ON and follow the prompts

# Heartsaver®
# Child CPR AED

*Tap and shout*

*Yell for help. Send someone
to phone 911 and get an AED*

*Look for no breathing or
only gasping*

*Push hard and fast.
Give 30 compressions*

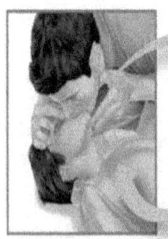
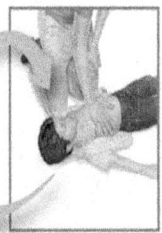

*Open the airway and give
2 breaths*

*Repeat sets of 30 compressions
and 2 breaths*

*If you are alone after 5 sets of
30 compressions and 2 breaths,
phone 911, and then resume
sets of 30:2*

*When the AED arrives, turn it
ON and follow the prompts*

## CHAPTER THREE – SHOTS

Obviously, this is something between you and your doctor. Tucker and I keep up to date on our Tetanus shots, Whooping Cough, Flu vaccines, and recently got Pneumonia and Shingles vaccines. Disease prevention is part of my ability to laugh at the days to come.

## CHAPTER FOUR – FOOD, BEYOND THE BASICS

### Meal in a Bag Dinner

NOTE: Buy each item on your ingredients list x10. Everything fits into your baggie except the bottled water. Be sure to buy 20 if an item (like 2 cans of potatoes) is doubled in the individual recipe. Have on hand at least as many on gallon freezer bags as dinners you are making up. Have on hand some sandwich bags also for loose ingredients you are measuring out (like onion flakes.)  Finally, write up each recipe once on recipe cards and photocopy each one so that you have a photocopied recipe card to place in each bag.

1. **<u>Prepper Rice and Beans with Tomato Cornbread Cakes</u>** (yum)
   To buy/ingredients:

   1 pkg. cornbread mix
   1 cup rice (I measure this and put it into a sandwich baggie.
   2 chicken bouillon cubes
   2 cans beans (I use pinto)
   1 14.5 oz. can diced tomatoes
   1 can whole kernel corn
   ¼ cup chili powder (again, just measure out into a sandwich baggie)
   1 Tablespoon onion flakes (in a baggie)
   1 16.5 oz bottled water (2 cups)

NOTE: This recipe and all that follow fit into a one gallon size zip lock type freezer bag.

To make:

Mix cornbread mix with the corn and tomatoes (including the liquids).  Cook as pancakes.  Make rice (2 cups water to 1 cup rice) with bullion added to the water.  Add beans and seasonings to cooked rice.


## 2. <u>Prepper Risotto with Beef and Red Wine</u>

To buy/ingredients:

1 can mushrooms
1 can roast beef
1 small jar Parmesan Cheese
1 can peas
1 box Rice a Roni (any flavor)
2 bottles (mini) red wine

To make:

Cook Rice a Roni according to instructions (brown it dry in a skillet if no butter or oil is available). Add wine and mushroom water and pea water to plain water to equal 2 ¼ cups.  Simmer after a one minute boil. Cover and cook 15-20 minutes.  Add beef and peas at the end.  Stir in gently.  Add entire package of parmesan cheese.  Stir in until it all melts.


## 3. <u>Prepper Beef Stew with Biscuits</u>

To buy/ingredients:

1 package egg noodles
1 can roast beef
1 can mushrooms
1 can sliced carrots
1 package cheesy-garlic biscuits mix (I get it
at Wal-Mart for a dollar)
1 package beef stew seasoning

To make:

Combine beef, mushrooms, carrots, and seasoning
with all liquids in the cans. Boil noodles in enough
water to cover (reserve water after cooking and
draining noodles.) Use water to make the biscuits
dough. Boil all the combined ingredients, then
simmer with drops of biscuit dough dropped on
top. Cover and simmer until dough is cooked.
About 10 minutes. Add in cooked noodles.

NOTE: In this recipe and many others here, a dutch
oven works great, especially over a camp fire.

### 4. <u>Prepper Ham and Scalloped Potatoes</u>

To buy/ingredients:

2 cans sliced potatoes
1 can evaporated milk
1 can peas
1 canned ham (small size)
1 McCormick's Four Cheese packet

To make:

Mix cheese packet with 1 can evaporated milk. (add water if needed.) Dice entire ham. In a pan or dutch oven create a bottom layer using 1/3$^{rd}$ of the potato slices, diced ham and peas. Pour 1/3$^{rd}$ of the cheese sauce over the bottom layer. Repeat twice more. Cover and bake. Again, the dutch oven allows you to bake this over a camp fire or even a bbq.

## 5. Prepper Chili

To buy/ingredients:

1 can diced tomatoes
1 can whole kernel corn or hominy

2 cans beans (pinto or kidney)
1 small can green chilies (mild)
1 cup rice
2 beef bouillon cubes
¼ taco seasoning
1/8 cup minced onions
1 16.5 oz bottle of water (2 cups)

To make:

Prepare rice with bouillon-flavored water. Add cooked rice to a pot in which you have added all your canned ingredients. Add minced onion and taco seasoning (or chili seasoning if you prefer.) Cook over low heat until desired thickness.

NOTE: I know traditional chili does not contain rice, but in the prepper chili I've added it for nutrition, bulk, and thickness. It tastes great!

## 6. Prepper Pesto Chicken Penne Pasta

To buy/ingredients:
1 box Penne pasta
1 small bottle Parmesan Cheese

1 jar Pesto
1 can cooked chicken
1 chicken bouillon cube (for added flavor, I buy the tomato/chicken cubes in the Mexican food section at Wal-Mart.)

To make:

Boil the pasta in bullion-flavored water. (10 minutes). Drain. Add the pesto, chicken, and all of the cheese. Stir gently until cheese is melted.

## 7. <u>Prepper Tuna with Broccoli and Mushroom Pasta</u>

To buy/ingredients:

1 jar Alfredo Sauce
3 cans tuna (I use in oil. In SHTF times, oils are hard to come by. Calories and fat are GOOD.)
1 can mushrooms
1 Alfredo sauce packet
1 box pasta (you choose)

To make:

Cook pasta and drain. (reserve water). Make Alfredo sauce packet using reserved water. Gently combine the pasta sauce you've made, with the cooked pasta and the jar of Alfredo sauce. Begin to simmer, then add the tuna (with the oil!) and mushrooms. Simmer until heated through (about 3 minutes.) So good and creamy.

## 8. Prepper Mac and Cheese with Chicken and Carrots

To buy/ingredients:

2 boxes macaroni and cheese
2 cans cooked chicken
1 can slice carrots

To make:

This is simple, but tasty and filling. Simply make up the mac and cheese box according to the directions (but don't worry if you have not butter, not needed). Add chicken and drained carrots. Mix gently. Reheat if needed.

## 9. Prepper Chop (Shepherd's Pie)

NOTE: We use our cobb oven or solar oven for this, but I know this also works on the bbq.

To buy/ingredients:

1 can cooked beef
1 can peas
2 pouches instant mashed potatoes
1 teaspoon paprika
1 cup dehydrated cheddar cheese (if available. We buy #10 cans from www.beprepared.com)

Prepare the mashed potatoes using the beef water and the pea's water and any additional plain water needed.  In a pan or dutch oven, layer the beef, peas, and mashed potatoes. Top with rehydrated cheese, if available. Bake about 20 minutes until thoroughly heated.

## 10.   Prepper Hawaiian Pizza

To buy/ingredients:

1 cup pineapple chunks
1 small canned ham
2 packets pizza crust mix
1 cup dehydrated cheese (if available in your preps)
1 can or jar of pizza/spaghetti sauce

Add water to pizza crust mix according to packet directions. Spread over a pizza pan. Bake on a closed bbq, or cobb oven or solar oven until done. Top with sauce, ham, cheese, pineapple. Return to bake until hot. (about 3 minutes)The cheese may not melt, but it still tastes amazing.

11.      Prepper Salmon and Rice

We call this pink rice!

To buy/ingredients:

1 can/jar mushrooms
6 packets soy sauce (saved from our many dinners out!)
2 cups rice
4 cups water (2 bottled water)

2 chicken bouillon cubes
1 can cream of chicken soup or cream of mushroom soup
1 can salmon
1 can spinach

Prepare rice in bouillon-flavored water and can of undiluted soup.
Add mushrooms, salmon, and spinach to the rice.  Reheat if necessary. Let each person add their own soy sauce.

FINAL NOTE: My focus is always on nutrition, including calories and fat (lots of both) and tastiness.  These recipes are representative of our family's tastes, yours may be entirely different.  Develop your own recipes!  Just be sure to keep within the parameters of that gallon bag and ease of preparation.

# EGGS

To purchase OvaEasy eggs, I go to www.rei.com.  At the time of this writing shipping is free if you spend over $50.00 and the price of the eggs goes down to $5.40 per dozen if you buy 6 packets (of one dozen eggs per packet.)  I order at least 10 dozen at a time (10 packets) for a total of $54.00!

## CHAPTER FIVE – FRUIT TREES

I have nothing to add to this chapter except to encourage you at home and on your refuge property to always be thinking of the "usefulness" of everything you plant.

That's not to say don't plant flowers (although many flowering plants are also useful, like lavender and rosemary.)  However, train yourself to have the mind-set of preparedness even as it extends to your garden.

Included below is list of what I think are useful trees for any garden, however, your location has EVERYTHING to do with your choices.  Here is a map of the United States and its planting zones.  Also, a great website with tree suggestions by region.  A good common sense approach also is to just look around your own neck of the woods.  Ask yourself, "What food producing trees grows best here?"

NOTE: Keep in mind that all fruit and nut-bearing trees will not give any fruit until they are at least five years of age. I learned in my Master Gardener training to buy the biggest/oldest fruit and nut tree I could afford (and that poor Tucker could manage to lift.)

http://www.raintreenursery.com/Regional_Plant s.html

http://planthardiness.ars.usda.gov/PHZMWeb/

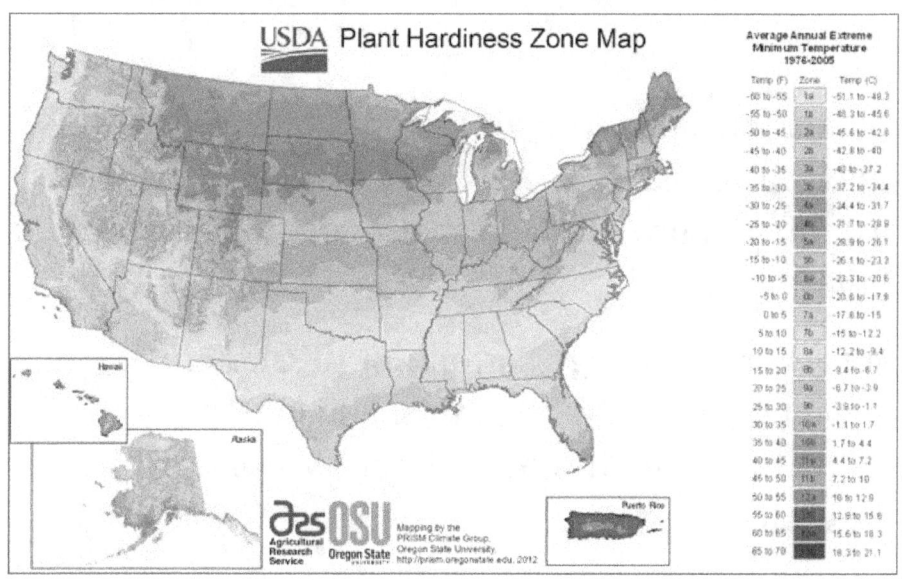

Recommended trees:

1. Apples and pears
2. Any stone fruit trees (cherry, plums, nectarines, apricots, etc.)
3. Nut trees (almonds, walnuts, pecans) – the bigger the better. (can take 15 (!) years to produce)
4. Citrus (which includes avocado). If you live in a cold winter climate, put your citrus trees in a large pot and bring it indoors for winter.

## CHAPTER SIX – FIRESTARTERS

Firestarters and a flint or matches makes for a much easier outdoor cooking environment. The last thing you want to do is struggle to get a fire going.

My favorites are egg carton/lint firestarters, cosmetic pad/wax firestarters, and cotton ball/petroleum jelly (name brand Vaseline) firestarter.

# EGG CARTON AND LINT FIRESTARTERS:

Ingredients:

1. An empty cardboard (not Styrofoam!) egg carton.
2. A old taper candle (or if you are a candle scrapper, like me, a bunch of used birthday candles)
3. Dryer lint

To make:

1. Open up your egg carton.
2. Using kitchen shears, cut off the top of the egg carton.
3. Stuff down as much dryer lint into each individual egg cup as will fit.
4. Carefully light a candle (away from the highly flammable lint) DO THIS IN THE SINK!!

5. Holding the candle at an angle, drip wax into each egg cup on top of the lint until the melted wax soaks into the lint and begins to cover it. (about 25 drops of wax from the candle)
6. Let the egg carton get cool and dry. Just walk away for a few minutes.
7. Carefully tear or cut each egg cup away until you have a dozen free little Firestarters!

Stuff the cups with cotton (mostly lint)

Melt wax 25-30 drops of wax in each cup

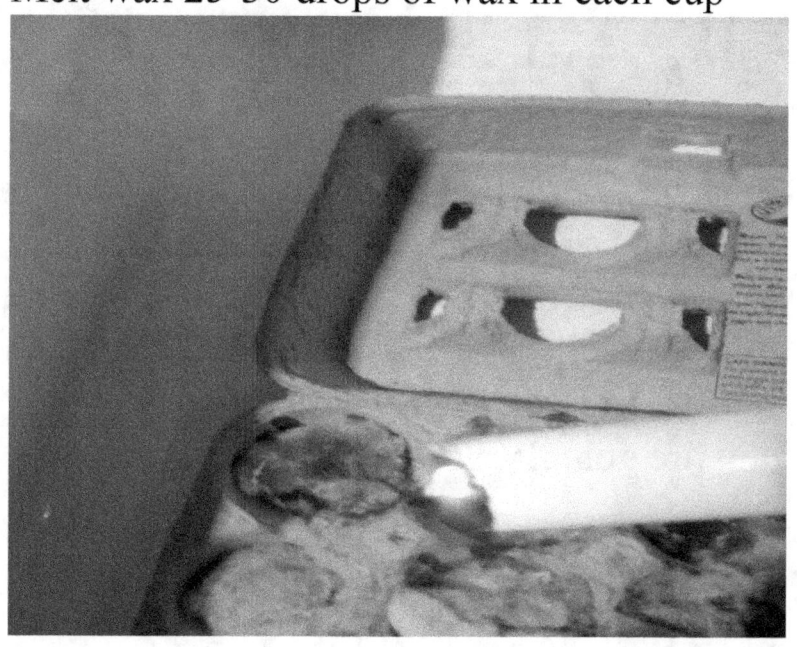

Cut and Store!

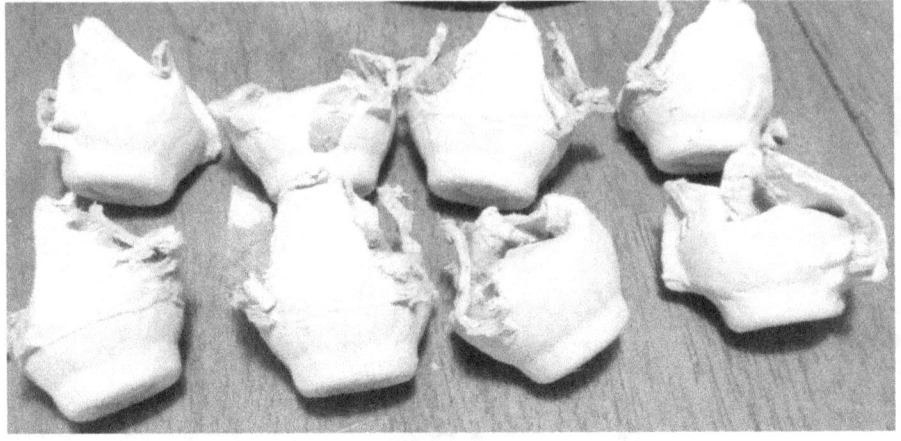

These little Firestarters will ignite easily with a flint or a match and can be used to start wood fires in your wood stove or campfire. They will burn at least 5 minutes with a very strong flame. More than long enough to get a fire going!

### Cotton Ball Firestarters

This firestarter is so easy! Go to the dollar store and buy a big container of petroleum jelly (generic Vaseline) and a couple of bags of cotton balls. Just store them together in a gallon size plastic bag.

All you have to do is dip a cotton ball into the petroleum jelly (a dap will do). A flint or a match will make a fire. Just put the soaked ball at the bottom of your kindling pile and set it on fire. Whoosh! Instant fire!

## Cosmetic Pads Firestarter

I buy makeup remover pads at the dollar store. You know those round or square all cotton things? They sell them in bags of 80-150 (depending on the shape) for a dollar. Each on makes one or two Firestarters, so they calculate out to a penny or so a piece. I use them the same way as the egg cup and cotton ball Firestarters. The nice thing about the cosmetic pad Firestarters is that the light even easier (if that's possible) than the other two. Once made, I tear one in half and all these little cotton fibers are exposed, just beggin' to be set fire.

Here's how I make them:

Only two ingredients: a cotton pad and wax. Those two ingredients, wax or parchment paper and a pot are all you need.

NOTE: I have a dedicated pan for melting wax because it's just too hard to clean out wax in a pot once it has been used to melt wax.

1. I take a quarter of a wax block (available at all craft stores and eBay and Amazon) and melt it slowly (keep your stove on the lowest setting.)
2. Take the pot off the stove and dip one half of the pad, then the other half until its covered in wax.
3. Lay each pad down on some wax paper and let cool.

    Then bag them in sandwich size bags (about 10 per baggie.)

You can easily make 100 in about thirty minutes.

NOTE ON STORING FIRESTARTERS:  You know those big red plastic rectangular tubs with lids that the big box stores (like Wal-Mart and K-Mart) sell at Christmas?  I have a big one that is clearly labelled "FIRE!" on all sides and the top using black permanent marker.  In it I store all my Firestarters, along with flints, matches, and BBQ lighters.  It's very easy to spot when fire is needed quick.


## CHAPTER SEVEN – ROOT CELLARS/COLD STORAGE

## Shipping Container Root Cellar

As you know, we backed two 20 foot containers in a hillside, backfilled the sides and back with soil, covered the top with heavy-duty tarp and insulation. Then we topped it off with a roof deck. The front is now faced with concrete block except for a door opening on each side.

I have heard of many folk burying their containers, but frankly, this makes me nervous. Tucker, my expert, tells me that the weight of all that soil could cause a cave-in. Research this for yourselves by going to www.google.com and typing shipping container root cellars. An image search on this subject is like eye-candy! So inspiring. A google search will open you up to dozens of survival forums discussing the how to's of this wonderful way to store.

We found our shipping containers at www.craigslist.com. We paid $1500 each including delivery. I suspect if we'd asked around more, we could have gotten a much better deal.

## Refrigerator, Freezers, Trash Can, and Ice Chest Root Cellar

This is so simple I'm embarrassed to give the instructions! All you do is dig a hole the size and depth of your container. Refrigerators and upright freezers laid on their backs and dropped into the hole. The doors are not submerged.

Chest freezers, trash cans and ice chests are simply dropped straight into the hole. Again, leave the top unburied.

Straw can be put on top of the lids or doors if you want more insulation.  If these are put into holes dug in the shade, the inside temperature should always be between 55 and 65 degrees.

## CHAPTER EIGHT – REFUGE LAND

Look for land that is off the beaten path.  That means far enough away from the city and jobs that it is unappealing for anyone looking for land that is commuting distance.

Look for land that is not off a main highway.  Look for land that is off a road that is off a road that is off a road…

The best place to find land is by doing local real estate searches on the internet.  For example, I might do a google search of "rural land" or "acreage" and "owner financing" and my region.

Don't go for ads that promote electricity or sewer systems.  You want land that is totally off grid.

Basically, raw land. Look for the opposite of Location, Location, Location! Look for a place that is not convenient to anything, but refuge.

## CHAPTER NINE – WELLS AND SPRINGS

### Wells

You can dig your own. Not only does this save thousands of dollars, but it gives you anonymity. No locals are aware of your activities if you lay low and do it yourself!

Here is the company that we got our well-drilling kit from: http://www.howtodrillawell.com/

### Springs

Tucker captures our season spring water every year and uses it to fill our 2500 and 3000 gallon tanks we have spread all over our refuge land.

Here's how he does it:

Tucker follows the stream uphill from our camp until he finds a modest waterfall (about six feet high). Then, he puts a large animal trough (black rubber kind) and drills a hole in the bottom front. He added fittings over the hole so that a garden hose could screw into the fittings. This type of drill bit and fitting is at your local hardware store. Go to a smaller store, those guys seem to know their stuff better than the employees and the giant hardware stores.

NOTE: We buy industrial type water hoses. Ours are a brownish red. The rubber is thicker and is of a material that won't degrade so quickly in outdoor environments.

Then he places the trough (with some heavy boulders inside it to keep it in place) under the falling water. As the running water fills and overfills the trough, the hose also fills with water which runs downstream and into our 2500 gallon water tank. Over the years we've added interconnecting 2500 - 3000 gallon tanks (each a bit downhill from each other) and they fill as the one above reaches capacity and overflows into another garden hose.

## CHAPTER TEN – HOW TO PICK YOUR GROUP

I'm not trying to be facetious when I say, PRAY. For those trying to get ahead of future problems, prayer is the best way to start. We can't know the future, but we know someone who does and it's Him we pray to. His name is Jesus.

I hesitate to say look for member at your church. If your church is a HAND (have a nice day) church, you will not be received well and you'll be spilling the beans when they change their minds and all rush to your not-so-secret refuge.

I don't think there is a magic formula. However, I've found a great deal of inspiration from a Christian end times writer, Kristin Wisen who wrote two wonderful novels that feature Christians coming together and forming refuge groups. Her books, only in hardback, (sigh) can be found here:

http://www.amazon.com/s/ref=dp_byline_sr_book_1?ie=UTF8&field-author=Kristen+Wisen&search-alias=books&text=Kristen+Wisen&sort=relevancerank

I also love a discussion group at

http://www.fulfilledprophecy.com/discussion/
You will find some lovely and intelligent Christian folks there. Some might just be local! ;)


## CHAPTER ELEVEN – HOMESCHOOL


If you are just now thinking about preparing for a time when there are children in your refuge group/camp, I suggest these wonderful groups on the internet:

http://www.hslda.org/LandingPages/local-groups.asp

http://homeedmag.com/groups


For curriculum ideas check these out (but don't think you need to buy their complete sets. I never do!)

http://www.sonlight.com/curriculum.html

http://www.aceministries.com/homeschool/

http://www.abeka.com/homeschool/

http://www.tapestryofgrace.com/index.php

Also, look at this wonderful company which guides kids through a year on the Prairie, and another year through Narnia!

http://cadroncreek.com/

NOTE: Once I find curriculum I always go buy it at www.christianbooks.com. The price is cheaper and a google of coupons for "christianbook.com coupons" always gets me a free shipping code!

Don't forget to pick up some good reference material for star-gazing, nature and plant study, and basic building ideas. Kids (and adults) love this stuff.

I can be reached at mrstuckerowen@hotmail.com

Love, Katie